MW00571157

Sayings
for
Teachers

Edited by David C. Jones

Detselig Enterprises Ltd.

Calgary, Alberta, Canada

©1997 David C. Jones

Canadian Cataloguing in Publication Data
Main entry under title:

Sayings for teachers

ISBN 1-55059-144-4
1. Teaching—Quotations, maxims, etc.   2. Teachers—Miscellanea.   I. Jones, David C., 1943-
   LB1027.S39 1997   371.1'02   C97-910026-7

Detselig Enterprises Ltd.
210, 1220 Kensington Rd. N.W.
Calgary, Alberta T2N 3P5

Detselig Enterprises Ltd. appreciates the financial
support for our 1997 publishing program, provided by
Canadian Heritage and the Alberta Foundation for the
Arts, a beneficiary of the Lottery Fund of the Govern-
ment of Alberta.

Printed in Canada   ISBN 1-55059-144-4
SAN 115-0324

Dedication

To the students who inspired these thoughts.

Introduction
We Are All Teachers

Everyone is a teacher, and in one way or another, everyone teaches all the time. Sadly, we are not always learners. "Personally, I am always ready to learn," said Winston Churchill, "although I do not always like being taught." "We might be more eager to accept good advice," added Leonard Levinson, "if it didn't continually interfere with our plans."

Readers may decide for themselves what is true in this little volume. But there is a process by which truth becomes known, Elbert Hubbard once revealed: "Truth, in its struggle for recognition, passes through four distinct stages. First, we say it is damnable, dangerous, disorderly, and will surely disrupt society. Second, we declare it heretical, infidelic, and contrary to the Bible. Third, we say it is really a matter of no importance either one way or the other. Fourth, we aver we have always upheld and believed it."

From this sparkling analysis, I am inclined to believe that to discount anything in this book is merely to be at one of the first three stages.

But then, W.H. Auden once said that "a professor is one who talks in someone else's sleep."

David C. Jones

Prologue

Nothing ever becomes real till it is experienced
– even a proverb is no proverb to you till your life
has illustrated it.

John Keats

A Teacher's Identity

There is no question but reflects this one. There is no conflict that does not entail the single, simple question, "What am I?"

Uncertainty about what you must be is self-deception on a scale so vast, its magnitude can hardly be conceived.

A Course in Miracles, V2, 260

Drink in the ozone, bathe in the sunshine, and out in the silent night, under the stars, say to yourself again and yet again, "I am a part of all my eyes behold!" And the feeling will surely come to you that you are no mere interloper between earth and sky; but that you are a necessary particle of the Whole.

Elbert Hubbard

God made the senses turn outwards; man therefore looks outwards, but not into himself. But occasionally a daring soul, desiring immortality, has looked back and found himself.

The Upanishads

A Teacher's First Principles

Any situation must be to you a chance to teach others what you are, and what they are to you. No more than that, but also never less.

A Course in Miracles, V3, 1

Everyone teaches, and teaches all the time. This is a responsibility you inevitably assume the moment you accept any premise at all, and no one can organize his life without some thought system. Once you have developed a thought system of any kind, you live by it and teach it. Your capacity for allegiance to a thought system may be misplaced, but it is still a form of faith and can be redirected.

Ibid., V1, 84

Everyone convinces you of what you want to perceive. . . . Everything you perceive is a witness to the thought system you want to be true.

Ibid., V1, 192

Remember always that what you believe, you will teach.

Ibid., V1, 86

If you react as if you are persecuted, you are teaching persecution.

Ibid., V1, 85

There is nothing noble in being superior to someone else. The true nobility is in being superior to your previous self.

Hindu proverb

When I do good, I feel good. When I do bad, I feel bad. That's my religion.

Abraham Lincoln

The good is what works is a sound though insufficient statement. Only the good *can* work. Nothing else works at all.

A Course in Miracles, V1, 161

Every good teacher hopes to give his students so much of his own learning that they will one day no longer need him. This is the one true goal of the teacher.

Ibid., V1, 48

Identify yourself with your high potential, not with your mistakes. To identify yourself with weakness, even in the name of self-honesty, is to accept weakness as your reality.

J. Donald Walters

Do not let what you cannot do interfere with what you can do.

John Wooden

All things worthwhile must be difficult. If it were easy to earn spiritual prizes they would not be worth having.

Silver Birch

The gem cannot be polished without friction, nor the person perfected without trials.

Chinese proverb

God offers to every mind its choice between truth and repose.

Ralph Waldo Emerson

Constantly be willing to reevaluate your first principles.

J. Donald Walters

A Teacher's Mistakes

The first problem for all of us, men and women, is not to learn but to unlearn.

Gloria Steinem

When somebody points out to you a mistake you have committed, and you recognize that he is right, don't blame yourself. Be grateful rather that now you can work to remove an impediment to your happiness. The impediment was there anyway; to recognize it is your good fortune.

When troubles beset you, seek both their cause and their solution in yourself. Never accept for yourself the victim's role.

J. Donald Walters

How to diminish in the eyes of your pupils? Play favorites, be inconsistent. Refuse to acknowledge an honest viewpoint, refuse to apologize when you know you are wrong, refuse to change your mind when you see the truth.

DCJ

Keep doing what you're doing and you'll keep getting what you're getting.

Johnny Harris

Warning to Students

Remember, no one can make you feel inferior without your consent.

Eleanor Roosevelt

A Teacher's Disappointments

Do you not see that all your misery comes from the strange belief that you are powerless?

A Course in Miracles, V1, 430

When you are weary, remember you have hurt yourself.

Ibid., V1, 184

When you are sad, know *this need not be*. Depression comes from a sense of being deprived of something you want and do not have. Remember that you are deprived of nothing except by your own decisions, and then decide otherwise.

Ibid., V1, 57

There is nothing so sad that good will not come of it.

Spanish proverb

You will learn to suffer less through sorrow and disappointment first by making fewer personal plans regarding other personalities, and second by accepting your lot when you have faithfully performed your duty.

The Urantia Book

No one who has escaped the world and all its ills looks back on it with condemnation.

A Course in Miracles, V3, 32

A Teacher's Stress

Burnout occurs when well-meaning teachers overextend their true responsibility, overcontrol the learning environment, and attack themselves for their students' mistakes.

DCJ

The time to relax is when you don't have time for it.

Sidney J. Harris

The higher the mortal species the greater the stress and the greater the capacity for humor as well as the necessity for it.

The Urantia Book

No one can create anger or stress within you. Only you can do that by virtue of how you process your world.

Wayne Dyer

That the birds of worry and care fly above your head, this you cannot change; but that they build nests in your hair, this you can prevent.

Chinese proverb

A Teacher's Anger

Anger cannot occur unless you believe that you have been attacked, that your attack is justified in return, and that you are in no way responsible for it. Given these three wholly irrational premises, the equally irrational conclusion that a brother is worthy of attack rather than of love must follow. What can be expected from insane premises except an insane conclusion?

A Course in Miracles, V1, 84

When you are angry, is it not because someone has failed to fill the function you allotted to him? And does not this become the "reason" your attack is justified?

Ibid., V1, 569

All anger is nothing more than an attempt to make someone feel guilty. . . .

Ibid., V1, 297

Perhaps it will be helpful to remember that no one can be angry at a fact. It is always an interpretation that gives rise to negative emotions, regardless of their seeming justification by what appears as facts.

Ibid., V3, 42

If anger comes from an interpretation and not a fact, it is never justified. Once this is even dimly grasped, the way is open. . . . The interpretation can be changed at last.

Ibid., V3, 44

The hate we sow finds lodgment in our hearts, and the crop is nettles that Fate unrelentingly demands we gather.

Elbert Hubbard

We can scarcely hate anyone that we know.

William Hazlitt

Speak when you are angry, and you will make the best speech you will ever regret.

Ambrose Bierce

A Teacher's Power

The highest manifestation of power is the deliberate refusal . . . to abuse it.

The weaknesses of many make the leader possible – and the man who craves disciples and wants followers is always more or less of a charlatan.

The man of genuine worth and insight wants to be himself; and he wants others to be themselves also.

Elbert Hubbard

A Teacher's Judgments

You are much more of what you *do not* understand about yourself than you are what you *do* understand about yourself.

Lazaris

What we humanely know is less than a billionth part of what we do not know. Yet that speck, which cannot support anything, is the foundation of all our judgments about everything.

DCJ

Everyone complains of his memory, but no one complains of his judgment.

François de la Rochefoucauld

The aim of our curriculum, unlike the goal of the world's learning, is the recognition that judgment in the usual sense is impossible. This is not an opinion, but a fact. In order to judge anything rightly, one would have to be fully aware of an inconceivably wide range of things; past, present, and to come. One would have to recognize in advance all the effects of his judgments on everyone and everything involved in them in any way. And one would have to be certain there is no distortion in his perception, so that his judgment would be wholly fair to everyone on whom it rests now, and in the future. Who is in a position to do this? Who except in grandiose fantasies would claim this for himself?

A Course in Miracles, V3, 26

Do not seek to discover or discuss the evil in others, for the attempt will tarnish your own minds.

Sathya Sai Baba

A person reveals his own character by the things he approves of or disapproves of in others. What you criticize in others is what you harbor in yourself.

J. Donald Walters

When you judge others, you do not define them, you define yourself.

Wayne Dyer

The unhappiness you feel as a teacher is a measure of the degree to which you attack, demean, and judge your students.

DCJ

Grading on the curve disrespects students and teachers, for it assumes a sameness across classes and instructors that does not exist. It is cynicism masquerading as science.

DCJ

A Teacher's Cynicism

Cynicism is the belief in the futility of human thought and endeavor. As a plan of action it is meaningless, because to a cynic nothing works; as a reflection on others it is degrading, because to a cynic all are fools; as a judgment on the cynic it is equally demeaning, because to believe in the futility of one's thought and endeavor is to believe in one's own impotence.

DCJ

A critic is a man who knows the way but can't drive the car.

Kenneth Tynan

Place perfectionism in a cynic, and you will produce the purest form of self-condemnation on the face of the earth. The fall-out is despair, sickness, insanity, even suicide.

DCJ

A cynic is a man who knows the price of everything and the value of nothing.

Oscar Wilde

How many pessimists end up by desiring the things they fear, in order to prove that they are right?

Robert Mallet

Thought to Avoid

There are more horses' asses in this world than there are horses.

John Peers and Gordon Bennett

A Teacher's Communication

Truth need not be shouted, unless, perhaps, to make it audible to a crowd. Truth should be stated sensitively. Usually, therefore, it should be understated.

Think *space* in your speech. Try not to crowd your ideas.

J. Donald Walters

Too much emphasis is no emphasis – raise your voice too loud and no one hears you. Hit too hard and you excite sympathy for your victim. Draw your indictment too sweeping and it becomes suspicious.

Elbert Hubbard

Never put more than twenty words on an overhead slide. Use graphics. If you want to lose the audience, show slides with columns of numbers.

Simplify, don't complicate – especially processes, procedures and policies.

Richard A. Moran

Everything should be made as simple as possible, but not one bit simpler.

Albert Einstein

He who conceals a useful truth is equally guilty with the propagator of an injurious falsehood.

St. Augustine

Look for concrete examples to illustrate your ideas. The more abstract a presentation, the less others will welcome it as true.

Temper the sword of reason in the fire of practicality. Ask of any idea not merely that it be reasonable, but that it work.

Don't think, "How can I do this differently?" Don't even think, "How can I do it better?" Think, "How should it be done?"

J. Donald Walters

Warning to Students

Plagiarist. One who gives birth to an adopted baby.

Anonymous

A Teacher's Leadership

Do not follow where the path may lead. . . . Go instead where there is no path and leave a trail.

Benjamin Franklin

A Teacher's Physical Fitness

Raise your level of energy. Exercise vigorously every day. Breathe deeply. Sit and stand erect. Eat properly – a preponderance of fresh fruit and vegetables, less meat. A healthy body filled with vitality makes for healthy mental attitudes.

J. Donald Walters

A Teacher's Play

If play is to be genuine it must be lighthearted and pursued without purpose. That is why we usually fail if we try to have fun.

Larry Dossey

A Teacher's Joy

People in the West are always getting ready to live.

Chinese proverb

Exult in your students' discoveries and in what students can teach you.

DCJ

Be a factor in the happiness of others. The only true happiness is that which never remains with oneself, but, as it is experienced, is passed on to others.

N. Sri Ram

You cannot experience real joy all by yourself. A solitary life is fatal to happiness.

The Urantia Book

The very joy derived from service reacts on the body and makes you free from disease.

Sathya Sai Baba

A Teacher's Sense of Humor

You grow up the day you have your first real laugh at yourself.

Ethel Barrymore

A Teacher's Gifts

Nothing, but nothing, can stop you from rendering the service for which you were born into this world.

Silver Birch

To give and to receive are one in truth. . . . Close your eyes, and for five minutes think of what you would hold out to everyone, to have it yours. You might, for instance, say:
"To everyone I offer quietness.
To everyone I offer peace of mind.
To everyone I offer gentleness."
Say each one slowly and then pause a while, expecting to receive the gift you gave. And it will come to you in the amount in which you gave it.

A Course in Miracles, V2, 192

You make attempts at kindness and forgiveness. Yet you turn them to attack again, unless you find external gratitude and lavish thanks. Your gifts must be received with honor, lest they be withdrawn.

Ibid., V2, 367

It does not matter if another thinks your gifts unworthy. In his mind there is a part that joins with yours in thanking you. It does not matter if your gifts seem lost and ineffectual. They are received where they are given.

Ibid., V2, 367

It is not the function of God's teachers to evaluate the outcome of their gifts. It is merely their function to give them. Once they have done that they have also given the outcome, for that is part of the gift. No one can give if he is concerned with the result of giving. That is a limitation on the giving itself, and neither the giver nor the receiver would have the gift. . . . Who gives a gift and then remains with it, to be sure it is used as the giver deems appropriate? Such is not giving but imprisoning.

Ibid., V3, 19

There is an infinity in each one of us to give. We have to discover the mode of giving it.

[Those] who want nothing can give all.

N. Sri Ram

Whatever you want from others – love, support, loyalty – *you* be the first to give.

J. Donald Walters

The gift of one's time, attended by the notion that it is costly, is no gift at all; it is "service" for a price, and thus no genuine service at all. The burden of cost is what weighs so heavily and fatigues. Teachers who lament the cost of compassion have sold it at a loss.

DCJ

Warning to Students

Teachers open the door; you enter by yourself.
                                    Florence Buege

Some Counsel on Character

If there is a sleazy thread in your character you will weave it into the fabric you are making.

Elbert Hubbard

It's extremely difficult to lead further than you have gone yourself.

Anonymous

Administrators, in choosing a colleague or teacher, always remember that the character of the person is worth ten times what he or she knows.

DCJ

Enthusiasm

Why is enthusiasm so valued in a teacher? Because it is the clearest and most exhilarating sign that the teacher is *alive*. On seeing such a one, the dispirited and the dejected instinctively know that *that* is how to live.

DCJ

Graciousness

You can cultivate gracefulness, but graciousness is the aroma of friendliness that emanates from a love saturated soul. Goodness always compels respect, but devoid of grace it often repels affection. Goodness is universally attractive only when it is gracious. It is effective only when it is attractive.

The Urantia Book

Friendliness

A choice to be unfriendly must be a decision either that other things are more valuable than kindness, or that the pupil is unworthy of it.

DCJ

Accept others as they are, and you will encounter friends wherever you go.

Develop a sense of community with others. See that community as consisting of more than your little family, more than your neighborhood, more than the town or city in which you live. Expand your sense of community to include, finally, the entire world.

J. Donald Walters

Tolerance

If he is right and I am wrong, I will concede to him; if he is wrong and I am right, I will tolerate him.

Chinese proverb

The more one knows the more tolerant one becomes.

DCJ

Humility

To be uncertain is to be uncomfortable, but to be certain is to be ridiculous.

Chinese proverb

Respect

The worst sin is the mutilation of a child's spirit.
Erik H. Erikson

Do not cause injury to anyone's self-respect intentionally or unintentionally.
Sathya Sai Baba

My approach is to address a fault without ever attacking a child's character.
Marva Collins

Seek always to discover what impedes students' understanding of themselves. That impediment is often their own judgment of themselves as something other than beings of innate sanctity and prodigious potential.

DCJ

If heaven made him, earth can make use of him.
Chinese proverb

Let the elephant fell the trees, let the bushpig dig the holes, let the mason wasp fill in the walls, let the giraffe put up the roof, then we'll have a house.

Zaire proverb

Discipline

There is a time to wink as well as to see.
                              Benjamin Franklin

Self-Control

Remain calm under attack, withholding recognition from comments that are made simply to offend.

Possess things as necessary, but let no thing possess you.

J. Donald Walters

There is no limit to the good you can do in this world, if you don't care who gets the credit.

Dorothy Riggs

Mastering others is strength
Mastering yourself is true power.

Tao Te Ching

Conflict is inevitable – violence is not.

Elizabeth Loescher

Self-Reliance

Stand by your perceptions of truth, by your own strength, by your own inner guidance. Don't make crutches of other people.

J. Donald Walters

To be thrown on one's own resources is to be cast in the very lap of fortune.

Benjamin Franklin

Concentration

Obstacles are what you see when you take your eyes off the goal.

Jeneane Behme

Encouragement

Support others in their worthwhile goals, and let them *feel* your support. Don't merely wave your abstract blessings.

J. Donald Walters

Patience

Everything must await the coming of its time. You are born into the world, but no amount of anxiety and no manifestation of impatience will help you to grow up.

The Urantia Book

Non Procrastination

Oh Lord, give me chastity and continence, but not yet.

St. Augustine

Moderation

Repeat a good piece of advice three times, and even a dog will get bored.

Chinese proverb

Open-mindeness

That is what learning is, you suddenly understand something you've understood all your life, but in a new way.

Doris Lessing

Justice

She who has a sense of justice which allows her to lord it over herself, to punish herself, and to extend no mercy or compassion for self, can do nothing more than apply that embryonic sense of rightness to others. She is what she is. And how she treats herself, so she will tend to treat others.

DCJ

Humanity

It is my personal approach that creates the climate. It is my daily mood that makes the weather. . . . I possess a tremendous power to make a child's life miserable or joyous. I can be a tool of torture or an instrument of inspiration. I can humiliate or humor, hurt or heal. In all situations, it is my response that decides whether a crisis will be escalated or de-escalated and a child humanized or de-humanized.

Haim Ginott

Balance

Wisdom is knowing what to do next, skill is knowing how to do it, and virtue is doing it.

David Starr Jordan

Courage

One does not discover new lands without consenting to lose sight of the shore for a very long time.

André Gide

Behold the turtle. He makes progress only when he sticks his neck out.

James Bryant Conant

Courage is rightly esteemed the first of human qualities, because . . . it is the quality which guarantees all others.

Never, never, never, never give up.

Winston Churchill

Thought to Avoid

I can answer you in two words. Im possible!
Sam Goldwyn

A Teacher's Love

If you develop love, you don't have to develop anything else.

Sathya Sai Baba

Love conquers that separation which is the root-cause of all misunderstanding and trouble.

N. Sri Ram

When you want only love you will see nothing else.

A Course in Miracles, V1, 215

Harmony is the way of love. Disharmony is the way of self-affirmation.

Paramhansa Yogananda

Love must express itself as service.

Being a good example is the best form of service.

Duty without love is deplorable;
Duty with love is desirable;
Love without duty is Divine.

Sathya Sai Baba

Treat a child as though he already is the person he's capable of becoming.

Haim Ginott

To be able to love a butterfly we must care for a few caterpillars.

Agnes Hillock

The one question that ought to be asked on a teaching application is: do you love children?

Marva Collins

If you choose to see yourself as unloving you will not be happy. You are condeming yourself and must therefore regard yourself as inadequate.

A Course in Miracles, V1, 164

Whenever you have a choice between being right and being kind, always choose kind.

Wayne Dyer

After a while you learn the subtle difference between holding a hand and chaining a soul.

Kara DiGiovanna

The Ideal Teacher

A teacher can never truly teach unless he is still learning himself. A lamp can never light another lamp unless it continues to burn its own flame. The teacher who has come to the end of his subject, who has no living traffic with his knowledge, but merely repeats his lesson to his students can only load their minds. He cannot quicken them. Truth not only must inform, but also inspire. If the inspiration dies out and the information only accumulates then truth loses its infinity. The greater part of our learning in the schools has been waste, because for most of our teachers their subjects are like dead specimens of once living things, with which they have a learned acquaintance but no communication of life and love.

Rabindranath Tagore

Children Learn What They Live

If a child lives with criticism, she learns to condemn.

If a child lives with hostility, she learns to fight.

If a child lives with ridicule, she learns to be shy.

If a child lives with shame, she learns to feel guilty.

If a child lives with tolerance, she learns to be patient.

If a child lives with encouragement, she learns confidence.

If a child lives with praise, she learns to appreciate.

If a child lives with fairness, she learns justice.

If a child lives with security, she learns to have faith.

If a child lives with approval, she learns to like herself.

If a child lives with acceptance and friendship, she learns to find love in the world.

Anonymous

Excellence

Excellence is millimeters and not miles.
From poor to good is great. From good to best is
   small.
From almost best to best sometimes not measur-
   able.
The man who leaps the highest leaps perhaps an
   inch
Above the runner-up. How glorious that inch
And that split-second longer in the air before the
   fall.

                                        Robert Francis

A Teacher's Mastery

How many master teachers are not masters of their curricula?

None.

DCJ

A Teacher's Evaluation

The most powerful and least used way to improve is to ask students regularly and appropriately what kind of teacher you have been.

If they think, rightly or wrongly, you have been unfair or inefficient, you must change. If they are right, change your approach; if they are wrong, clarify it.

DCJ

A Teacher's Prayer

I do not want the peace which passeth understanding; I want the understanding which bringeth peace.

Helen Keller

Epilogue

We always say that at the end of your earthly term, if you have helped one soul to find itself, then your existence has been worthwhile.

Silver Birch